The Pied Piper

A Musical Play by

David Wood and
Dave and Toni Arthur

Based on the traditional tale made famous by Robert Browning

Samuel French - London
New York - Toronto - Hollywood

THE PIED PIPER

Commissioned by Orchard Theatre and Plymouth Theatre Royal, *The Pied Piper* was first produced by Orchard Theatre at the Octagon Theatre, Yeovil on 16th November, 1988; the production then toured the West of England, including a Christmas season at the Drum, Plymouth Theatre Royal. The cast was as follows:

The Mayor	Geoffrey Andrews
The Tradesman	Richard Deen
The Policeman	Simon Egerton
The Vicar	Simon Fielder
The Lame Child	Suzanne Gabriel
The Pied Piper	Peter Leafe
The Mother	Gill Nathanson
The Lollipop Lady	Krissy Wilson

Approximately 20 children were recruited at each theatre to play the Children of Hamelin

Director	Nigel Bryant
Assistant Director	Suzanne Gabriel
Designer	Anne Curry
Musical Director	Alan Ellis
Choreographer	Sue Harris

CHARACTERS

The play has been written for a minimum of eight actors, plus twenty children.

One actress plays a child. She can therefore act as a **Child Leader** in spoken choruses.

The suggested casting and role distribution is as follows:

Actor 1 (M): **The Pied Piper**
Actor 2 (M): **Business Man/Mayor**
Actor 3 (F) : **Mother/Maid**
Actor 4 (F) : **Child Leader/Lame Child**
Actor 5 (M): **Policeman/Constable/Old Rat**
Actor 6 (M): **Vicar/Priest**
Actor 7 (F) : **Lollipop Lady/Townsperson/Main Narrator**
Actor 8 (M): **Tradesman/Ratcatcher**

In the script, certain speeches are given to "**Narrator**" or "**Voice**". These speeches can be spoken individually or in chorus, divided up as the director sees fit. Some narration passages may benefit by the cast taking a line each; others may need the continuity of one speaker. It is suggested that if any actor has more narration than the others, it should be the **Lollipop Lady**.

PRODUCTION NOTES

Setting

The play takes place in Pied Piper's Street, Hamelin, but little or no attempt should be made to depict this naturalistically. The play could well be played on an empty stage with a colour-changing cyclorama or representational skyline of shopfronts, but these should not be practical or too detailed. Lighting is probably more important to the play than set. Atmosphere created with light will contribute much more than scenery.

Costumes and Props

The **Piper** is dressed throughout in a medieval costume, one side yellow and the other side red. This scheme is echoed on his face. The idea is for him to look feasible both as the original Pied Piper and also as an outlandishly dressed modern busker.

The **Townsfolk** are in modern dress, according to their occupation. It is an early summer's day, so the **Policeman** could be in shirtsleeves. In the "play within a play" the **Townsfolk** improvise the odd costume feature to identify them as their medieval counterparts. For example, the **Business Man** uses his bicycle chain and padlock for the **Mayor**'s chain of office. The **Tradesman**'s toolbox becomes the **Ratcatcher**'s trap.

The only "special" prop for the "play within a play" is, it is suggested, a rat half-mask for the **Old Rat**. The **Policeman** needs a truncheon and a whistle. The **Lollipop Lady**'s "lollipop stick" has, on one side, the **Ratcatcher**'s trade sign.

The **Children** are in modern dress, with grey, black or brown "tops" over T-shirts. They pull these over their heads to "become" rats. One child has a pogo stick, which becomes the **Lame Child**'s crutch. Another child pushes a doll's pram. In the "play within a play", the **Children** wear white nightshirts.

MUSICAL NUMBERS

ACT I

	Overture—*Pied Piper Theme* (Music 11)	
1.	Eerie minor version of *Boys and Girls Come out to Play*	The Piper (on pipe)
1a.	Nursery Rhymes—*Hickory, Dickory, Dock*/*Three Blind Mice*	Children
1b.	*Rats, Rats, Rats*	Children
1c.	Nursery Rhyme—*Ring a Ring of Roses*	Children
2.	Major version of *Boys and Girls Come Out to Play*	The Piper (on pipe)
3.	Dance version of *Boys and Girls Come Out to Play*	
4.	Fanfare to announce the story-telling	
4a.	Narration music	
5.	*One Foot Up and One Foot Down*	Townsfolk
6a & b.	Rats rhythm of rhymes	Children
7.	*Shhhhh!*	Townsfolk
8.	Fanfare, church music-like, to introduce Priest	
9.	Fanfare, as Ratcatcher fetches pot and brush	
10.	Minor version of *Boys and Girls Come Out to Play* (not on pipe)	
11.	*The Pied Piper's Song*	The Piper
12.	*Listen to the Music*	Rats
13.	*One Foot Up and One Foot Down* (reprise)	Townsfolk
13a.	Reprise last segment *Listen to the Music*	Old Rat
14.	Reprise chorus of *The Pied Piper's Song*	The Piper

ACT II

15.	*We Can Whistle, We Can Play*	Townsfolk
15a.	Electronic sounds	
16.	*One Foot Up and One Foot Down* (reprise)	Townsfolk
17.	Minor version of *Boys and Girls Come Out to Play*	The Piper,
18.	Major version of *Boys and Girls Come Out to Play*	Lame Child, Children
19.	*Mother's Lament*	Mother, Townsfolk

20.	Incidental music as Children enter	
21.	*Mother's Lament* (reprise)	Lame Child
22.	Electronic sound for tension	
23.	*Boys and Girls Come Out to Play*—dance version	The Piper (on pipe)
24.	Major version of *Boys and Girls Come out to Play*	The Piper (on pipe or recorded)
25.	Reprise chorus of *The Pied Piper's Song*	The Piper
26.	*We Can Whistle, We Can Play* (reprise) or: Suggested medley of reprises from *Boys and Girls Come Out to Play, We Can Whistle, We Can Sing, One Foot Up and One Foot Down, The Pied Piper's Song*	Company

NB. Other incidental music may be required.

Drumrolls are often suggested for tension or to introduce characters or to accompany mimed scenes—these could be "from the pit", or the actors could play them onstage as part of the action.

The piano/vocal score is available on sale from Samuel French Ltd.

ACT I

OVERTURE: Pied Piper Theme

Opening sequence. The Pied Piper is discovered centre stage with his back to the audience. Very subdued blue lighting which creates a silhouette effect

Music 1

The Piper plays a slow and eerie minor version of "Boys and Girls Come Out to Play" on his pipe, still with his back to the audience. He plays one complete verse

Children, including the Actor/Child Leader, enter

The Children and the Child Leader perform a stylized, slow, dream-like dance around the Piper, as though under his spell. When the second verse is finished, the Children break into two groups either side of the Piper and start, very quietly, to sing. This can be very simple, or involve overlapping counterpoint

Music 1a

Children, Group One

> Hickory dickory dock
> The mouse ran up the clock
> The clock struck one
> The mouse ran down
> Hickory dickory dock.

This is repeated in canon

Children, Group Two

> Three blind mice
> Three blind mice
> See how they run
> See how they run
> They all ran after the farmer's wife,
> Who cut off their tails with a carving knife
> Did you ever see such a thing in your life
> As three blind mice.

This is combined with Group One repeating "Hickory Dickory Dock"

All the children then get together in a huddle and whisper, not sing the following

Music 1b

Children (*whispering*)

> Rats, rats, rats,
> Some of them as big as cats
> Rats, rats, rats.
> First of all they give you fleas,
> Then they make you sneeze, sneeze, sneeze.
> Rats, rats, rats.

The Children then rise quite slowly and perform a ring dance

Music 1c

> Ring a ring of roses
> A pocket full of posies
> Atishoo, atishoo,
> We all fall down.

As the Children fall down they all expel a great sigh, which is picked up by a strange, electronic sound. As the sound gets louder and more perturbing the Lights fade down to Black-out

The Children exit

Black-out. After a pause, the lighting fades up to bright daylight

The Piper slowly turns round to face the audience in a less sinister way

Music 2

The Piper plays a major tune version of "Boys and Girls Come Out to Play". (In the original production this was made overtly contemporary with the Piper playing to accompaniment from a "ghetto-blaster" cassette player)

The Children including the Child Leader dash in again and start to dance in a modern energetic but not choreographed manner. One of the children hops in on a pogo stick, another pushes a doll's pram. Both abandon the toys to join the dance

Music 3

The Children and Child Leader dance

After a while, one by one the Townsfolk enter, as though on a shopping street. A Mother, A Vicar, A Business Man in a suit, a Lollipop Lady and a boiler-suited Tradesman

The Business Man arrives on his bicycle, perhaps through the auditorium. The Lollipop Lady carries her "lollipop stick". The Tradesman carries a wooden toolbox

They stand and watch, worried and shocked by the Children's behaviour; one or two attempt to stop the dancing, but fail. The Business Man acts firmly. He leaves his bicycle to one side and takes command

Business Man Stop! Stop this at once! All of you! Stop it!

The Piper stops playing and smiles enigmatically. The Children reluctantly stop dancing

Mother (*grabbing her two children*) Come away, you two. I don't know what's come over you.

Child Leader It's the music, the music. (*Turning to the Piper*) Play, play, play, play!

Children (*joining in with the chant*) Play, play, play, play!

The Policeman enters. He surveys the scene, then blows his whistle

The Children stop chanting

Policeman That's better. Now what on earth's going on?

Vicar The children were dancing, officer.

Lollipop Lady To the music.

Policeman Music? What music?

Piper (*calmly, with control*) My music.

All turn to the Piper

Policeman And who might you be?

Piper An honest musician, sir, earning an honest penny.

Policeman I think you'd better move on, me lad!

Piper Why?

Policeman You're creating a disturbance, that's why!

Piper (*seriously*) No sir, I create only Music. Merriment. Life.

The Children cheer

Business Man (*authoritatively*) Not *here* you don't!

Piper (*enigmatically*) Here, there and everywhere.

Policeman Look, there's no busking allowed here; there's a by-law against it. Understand?

Lollipop Lady That's right. No singing and dancing on *this* street. It's bad luck.

Vicar It goes back a long time. For hundreds of years music's been banned on this street.

Mother No singing.

Business Man No dancing.

Tradesman No nothing!

Lollipop Lady That's right; and especially no *children* dancing. You children should know that.

Child Leader Sorry. We forgot. We got carried away.

Small Child I don't know. No-one's ever told me why.

The Townsfolk exchange glances

Policeman Shall we tell her why?

Vicar I think we should.

Business Man It's our duty to explain.

Mother Every child must be warned.

Lollipop Lady Every child must be told.
Tradesman Every child *will* be told!

Music 4

Musical fanfare. The Children cheer and take their positions for the forthcoming story-telling. The Townsfolk sit the Small Child and the Piper as spectators. As the music ends, the Narrator/s step forward

Narrator The story starts long, long ago, when every one was happy. In those days, this street echoed to the sounds of music . . .

Music 4a

Drum beat

Hamelin Town's in Brunswick
By famous Hanover city
The river Weser deep and wide
Washes its walls on the southern side
A pleasanter spot you never spied.

Church bells ring out and music explodes into a lively dance song. The Children clap along

Music 5: One Foot Up and One Foot Down

Townsfolk

There's a law in Hamelin Town
That none of us should wear a frown
We laugh all day and sing and play
And down by the river we stroll and say

Chorus
One foot up and one foot down
That's the way in Hamelin Town
Life's too short to work all day
All we do is sing and play
So join our dance in Hamelin Town
One foot up and one foot down.

Church bells join in chiming

When the summer sun shines down
On the folk of Hamelin Town
We all join hands and form a ring
And as we dance we loudly sing
Hamelin Town!

Chorus

Dance

When the moon shines bright as day
All the shadows are chased away
Then old and young we all leap out
And through the streets we dance and shout
Hamelin Town!

Chorus

The Townsfolk hold their end-of-song/dance pose. The bells that have peeled before, change to death knell toll. The Lighting dims as the narration starts again

Narrator   But while the townsfolk danced and sang
                      The finger of fate was beckoning
                      In sombre mood the church bell rang
                      To announce their day of reckoning.
                      First an eerie squeaking sound
                      Filled the townsfolks' ears,
                      Then a scuffling on the ground
                      Confirmed their growing fears,
                      Suddenly a fearsome creature
                      Scuttled through the house.

A Child scuttles in and "becomes" a Rat pulling his/her top over his/her head and wiggling fingers as whiskers

                      Fleet of foot and furry of feature
                      Looking like a giant mouse.
                      Such a sight they'd never spied
                      How had such a thing occurred?
                      Women trembled, grown men cried,
                      "There's a second!", "There's a third!"

Two more Children scuttle on and "become" Rats

                      "Are we dreaming?" Children screaming
                      "Leave your homes and wake the cats!"
                      But outside the streets were teeming
                      With a loathsome plague of rats.

Music 6

Drum beat as the three Rats are joined by the other Children, also "becoming" Rats as they join in a cluster

The Rats suddenly tap the Townsfolk on the shoulders

The Townsfolk jump, react and dash off

The Rats are alone on stage

Music 6a

To drum accompaniment. Scuffling noises using feet (this should be about 8 beats). Squeaking noises (also 8 beats). Footsteps, running-on spot noises building to a climax (probably 16 beats)

After a silent pause ... the Rats divide vocally, but not physically, into two groups

Music 6b

Group One   Rumble, rumble,
                      Mutter, mutter, mumble,
                      Tumble, jumble,
                      Eek! Eek! Eek!

> Sniffle, snuffle,
> Riffle, ruffle, shuffle,
> Scuttle, scuffle,
> Eek! Eek! Eek!

Group Two   Great rats, small rats, lean rats, brawny rats.
Brown rats, black rats, grey rats, tawny rats.

Both groups together, Group Two dominant

Group One	**Group Two**
Rumble, rumble,	Great rats,
Mutter, mutter, mumble,	Small rats,
Tumble, jumble,	Lean rats,
Eek! Eek! Eek!	Brawny rats.
Sniffle, snuffle,	Brown rats,
Riffle, ruffle, shuffle,	Black rats,
Scuttle, scuffle,	Grey rats,
Eek! Eek! Eek!	Tawny rats.

Group Two   Rustle, scurry,
Hustle, bustle, hurry,
Helter skelter,
Eek! Eek! Eek!

Rabble, scrabble,
Gabble, babble, babble,
Scramble, scamper,
Eek! Eek! Eek!

Group One   Fast rats, slow rats, sleek rats, slimy rats,
Plump rats, thin rats, fierce rats, grimy rats.

Both groups together, Group One dominant

Group One	**Group Two**
Fast rats,	Rustle, scurry,
Slow rats,	Hustle, bustle, hurry,
Sleek rats,	Helter, skelter,
Slimy rats.	Eek! Eek! Eek!
Plump rats,	Rabble, scrabble,
Thin rats,	Gabble, babble, babble,
Fierce rats,	Scramble, scamper,
Grimy rats.	Eek! Eek! Eek!

Group One	Grey old plodders
Group Two	Gay young friskers
Group One	Fathers, mothers
Group Two	Uncles, cousins
Both Groups	Cocking tails and pricking whiskers
	Families by tens and dozens.

All together, getting faster

Group One	**Group Two**
Rumble, rumble,	Great rats,
Mutter, mutter, mumble,	Small rats,
Tumble, jumble,	Lean rats,
Eeek! Eek! Eek!	Brawny rats.
Sniffle, snuffle,	Brown rats,
Riffle, ruffle, shuffle,	Black rats,
Scuttle, scuffle,	Grey rats,
Eek! Eek! Eek!	Tawny rats.

Group One	Rats in packs and rats in pairs
Group Two	Rats of every shape and size
Both Groups	In the doors and up the stairs
	Take the Townsfolk by surprise.

Both groups together getting faster still

Group One	**Group Two**
Fast rats,	Rustle, scurry,
Slow rats,	Hustle, bustle, hurry,
Sleek rats,	Helter, skelter,
Slimy rats.	Eek, Eek! Eeek!
Plump rats,	Rabble, scrabble,
Thin rats,	Gabble, babble, babble,
Fierce rats,	Scramble, scamper,
Grimy rats.	Eek! Eek! Eek!

Both Groups   Rats, rats, rats, rats,
(*rising to a climax*) Rats, rats, rats, rats!

Black-out

The Rats exit

The Lights come back up

The Townsfolk enter and narrate as well as participate in the following mimed sequences with the Rats

Narrator   They fought the dogs and chased the cats

Drumroll. Three or four Townsfolk mime cats and dogs, mewing, barking, playing, sniffing, etc. . . .

Several Rats enter

The Rats, in an amusing pantomimic fashion, attack the dogs and cats, who eventually turn tail and exit pursued by the Rats

They snatched the babies from the cradles,

Drumroll. The Mother pushes a doll's pram, which has been left on the stage from the opening scene

More Rats enter

*One Rat diverts her; another takes a doll from the pram. The Rats use the doll
for a catching game*

> *The Mother looks aghast. Finally she manages to catch the doll and replace
> it in the pram before being chased off by the Rats*

>> They ate the cheese out of the vats
>> And licked the soup from the cooks' own ladles . . .

Drumroll

More Rats enter

The Townsfolk mime cooking with utensils

> *Rats enter and push them aside, then mime eating, getting fat, etc.*

> *The cooks flee*

The gorging Rats remain

>> They even spoiled the women's chats . . .

Two women mime an animated conversation

>> By drowning their speaking
>> With shrieking and squeaking
>> In fifty different sharps and flats . . .

Drumroll. The Rats see the women, and beckon on all the other Rats

> *The rest of the Rats enter*

*They advance behind the unsuspecting, chatting women, then start squeaking.
The women react as the Rats begin to circle round them, squeaking louder and
louder. Eventually the women scream in frustration. The squeaking stops*

Women   To cap it all these noisy rats
               Made nests inside our Sunday hats . . .

Two Rats mime taking off the women's hats

> *The women scream and retreat*

*The Rats, all fat and full, mime happily going to sleep. They lie on the floor
virtually covering the stage. They snore*

> *The Townsfolk enter warily, tiptoeing between sleeping Rats*

Music 7: Shhhhh!

Men   What can we do about—?
Women   Shhhhhh! Don't waken them!
Men   Who's going to help us out?
Women   Shhhhhh!
Men   Our world's turned inside out.
Women   Shhhhh! Don't waken them!
Men   Who can we tell about?

Women	Shhhhhhhhh!

We know we mustn't create a fuss
It's us kill them or them kill us
We're plagued by them
Afraid of them
We're plagued by them

Men	There's a curse upon the town
Women	Shhhhh! Don't waken them!

The leader of the Rats lifts his head a little, sniffs, twitches and falls back to sleep

Men	Scaly, furry, grey and brown
Women	Shhhhh!
Men	Our world's turned upside down
Women	Shhhhh! Don't waken them!
Men	Why don't they go and drown?
Women	Shhhhhhhhh!

They're quite appalling and crawling with fleas
And fleas, we've read, can spread disease
We're plagued by them
Afraid of them
We're plagued by them

Men	Poisons, potions even charms,
Women	Shhhhh! Don't waken them!
Men	Nothing seems to do them harm
Women	Shhhh!
Men	How can anyone keep calm?
Women	Shhhh! Don't waken them!
Men	When we're filled with such alarm?
Women	Shhhhh!
Men	Our cupboards all are bare
Women	Shhhh! Don't waken them!
Men	We're tearing out our hair
Women	Shhhhh!
Men	We've given up on prayer
Women	Shhhhh! Don't waken them!
Men	We're off to see the Mayor
Men **Women** }	(*together, shouting*) Now!
Rats (*waking up, aggressively*) Shhhhh!	

The Rats jump up and chase the Townsfolk off

The Business Man walks on and "becomes" Mayor by placing a padlock and chain from his bicycle around his neck

Mayor	I am the Mayor of this town
	I wear a chain and a fancy gown

	That I'm important there's no doubt
	I like rich food
Voice (*off*)	That's why he's stout
Mayor	Oysters, quails and breast of swan
	Are what I like to dine upon
	And at noon my paunch grows mutinous
	For a plate of turtle, green and glutinous.

A Maid enters

The Maid mimes carrying a very heavy tray, and puts it down in front of the Mayor, who mimes sitting

The Maid exits

Mayor   It's here! Bad luck, I've none to spare!
               I do enjoy it being Mayor.

He mimes tucking a bib into his collar, and prepares to eat, lifting a mimed knife and fork ...

Drumroll

Rats enter

Rats mime whisking away the tray from under the Mayor's nose. They hide behind him. The Mayor brings down the knife and fork with relish, stabbing his knees. He reacts in pain

The Rats pop out and rough him up, before dashing off

               Aaaaaaaaargh! Rats!!!

He stamps ineffectually

Townsfolk enter narrating as they walk

Narrator   At last the people in a body
               To the Town Hall came flocking
               'Tis clear to us our Mayor's a noddy
               Listen sir, we find it shocking
               To think we bought a gown of ermine
               For a dolt that can't determine
               How to rid us of our vermin.
               Rouse up, sir, give your brain a racking
               To find the remedy we're lacking
               Or, sure as fate, we'll send you packing!

After a pause ...

Mayor   It's easy to bid one rack one's brain
               I'm sure my poor head aches again
               I've scratched it so and all in vain
               Let's ask the priest, perhaps he'll know
               How best to fight the fearsome foe
               How best to make these vermin go.

The Vicar "becomes" the Priest

Music 8

Church-music-like fanfare

Priest   I can offer no solution
The rats are God's just retribution
A punishment for all your greed
Now drink and pleasure's become your creed.
You dance, you sing, you have no cares
And when did you last say your prayers?
From paths of righteousness you've strayed
And now the price needs must be paid
God decreed these furry creatures
Should become your moral teachers
Forsake enjoyment and high living
Then feel God's mercy all-forgiving
Turn your hearts to truth and virtue
And the rats will never hurt you.

The Townsfolk fall to their knees

Townsfolk   We repent! We're on our knees!
We repent! Now help us please!
Priest   See, Lord, see your children praying
(sincerely)   Hear, Lord, hear the words they're saying
From their plight may they be freed ...
Send help in this their hour of need.

Drumroll

The Tradesman stands up and "becomes" Ratcatcher, striking a heroic pose

Ratcatcher   My name's Rat-a-tat-tat
Roll up! Roll up!
Leave your houses
Leave your flats
I'm the famous Rat-a-tat-tat
Roll up! Roll up!

The Townsfolk turn and face him; the Lollipop Lady gives him her "lollipop"
stick

Now I hear you've got a problem
And I'm sure that I can help
Townsfolk
(in chorus)   He is sure that he can help us
Ratcatcher   Yes I am.
For I'm a paid up member
Of the Guild of Rodent Operatives

He turns the "lollipop" stick round to reveal the Ratcatcher's trade sign

No rat nor mouse has ever beaten me
With my cheese

He mimes holding cheese

Townsfolk   Phew!
Ratcatcher   And trap ...

He mimes holding a trap. A Townsperson runs to pick up his tool box left on the stage. He gives this to the Ratcatcher as a trap. The Ratcatcher shows a sign of appreciation

And faithful cat

The Ratcatcher smiles at this. A Townsperson runs off to the wings. Mewing is heard off-stage. The Townsperson runs back in, lovingly stroking a stuffed cat, which he hands to the Ratcatcher. The Ratcatcher smiles

With my cheese and trap and faithful cat
I'll clear your town as quick as that,

He clicks his fingers

And then from all your troubles you'll be free.
Townsfolk   And then from all our troubles we'll be free.

The Townsfolk cheer and clap

Mayor   I fear you underestimate
The problem that we contemplate
We're talking of a *hundred thousand* rats.
Ratcatcher   A hundred thousand did you say?
Why, that should take but ... half a day
I wouldn't even need to use the cat.
Townsfolk   He wouldn't even need to use his cat.
Ratcatcher   I've got this special smelly cheese
Townsfolk   Phew!!
Ratcatcher   The rats can sniff it on the breeze
So I place it "thus" within my *special* trap

He demonstrates setting up the rat-trap

Then when the stupid rats go in
And step upon this plate of tin
A little spring then closes up the flap.

He demonstrates this and gets his finger caught

Ouch!
Townsfolk   A little spring then closes up the flap.
1st Voice   He's a fraud and he's a faker
Ratcatcher   I think *you're* a trouble-maker
1st Voice   Catch a rat! He couldn't even catch the flu.
Ratcatcher   Well, yes, I made a mess of that,
But you should really see my cat,

And if *he* don't work, I'll ...
Spread the streets with glue!

Townsfolk   If his cat don't work he'll spread the streets with glue!

The Townsfolk laugh

Ratcatcher   I'll place the cat down nice and steady
When the rats come he'll be ready
He's braver than a lion and fighting fit
And woe betide the foolish rat.
That faces up to my old cat
He'll tear him into forty thousand bits.

Townsfolk   He'll tear him into forty thousand bits.

Drum roll, which continues as the Ratcatcher places the cat on the ground

Ratcatcher   Stand firm, stand firm my noble puss
Our future is in your paws

To Townsfolk

Stand back! Stand back! and give him room
To use his fearsome claws.

The drumroll increases in intensity as a Rat enters

The Rat advances slowly on the cat, and as the Rat touches noses with the cat, the Rat squeaks, and the cat with a loud mew, flies backwards into the wings, pulled on an invisible thread. The drum stops

The Rat exits

Townsfolk   Boo!
Mayor   Be off you fraud
Voice   The Mayor did shout
Townsfolk   Get out! Get out! Get out! Get out!

The Ratcatcher starts to go, then turns

Ratcatcher   Now hang about, don't jeer and scoff,
I promised you I'd see 'em off,
And see 'em off I guarantee I can!
The trap, the cat, the smelly cheese
Were but a prologue, if you please—
I now present to you—my masterplan!

All   He now presents to us his masterplan!

Music 9

Fanfare, as the Ratcatcher fetches a pot and brush

Ratcatcher   I proudly introduce to you
(*Revealing it*)
My pot of glue!
Townspeople   (*disparagingly*) Oh not the glue!

Ratcatcher	No, listen, 'cos its powers are quite unique
	Each whisker, tip of tail or claw
	In *this* gets stuck for evermore
	And soon you'll never hear another squeak!
All	And soon we'll never hear another squeak!
Ratcatcher	(*preparing*) So stand by ladies, stand by gents
	With skill my brush I fill
	You'll see me spread it on the street
	And then you'll see ... the kill!

Tension music

The Rats run on and cause chaos

During the chaos, the Ratcatcher sticks to his brush and finds the glue pot on his head

All	Boo!
Mayor	Be off you cheat!
Voice	The Mayor did shout.
All	Get out, get out, get out, get out!

The Ratcatcher makes an unceremonious exit

The Children rush back on and join in the booing

The Tradesman joins as soon as possible

Mayor	Oh! for a good efficient trap!

The Children face the audience and take up the narration

Children	Just as he said this what should hap
	At the chamber door, but a gentle tap?

Music 10

Three taps on a wood block introduce the minor version of "Boys and Girls". It is not, however, played on the pipe, but on another instrument. The tune is played throughout the following narration

Mayor	Come in!
Children	The Mayor cried, looking bigger,
	And in did come the strangest figure
	His queer long coat from heel to head
	Was half of yellow, half of red.

The Children look around for someone to play the Piper. Drum roll as they point to the Busker and beckon him to join them. All applaud as the Piper stands up and the Townsfolk clear a space to give him prominence. The Children sit downstage

No tuft on cheek nor beard on chin
But lips where smiles went out and in
There was no guessing his kith and kin

And nobody could enough admire
This curious man and his quaint attire.
And his fingers they were ever straying
As if impatient to be playing
Upon his pipe as low it dangled
Over his vesture so old-fangled.

Piper *(entering* If it please your honours?
into the spirit   **Music 11: The Pied Piper's Song**
of the story)

The Piper gives a stylized bow

(*Singing*)   I with a secret charm can draw
All creatures living beneath the sun
That creep or swim or fly or run
After me—so as you never saw.

And I chiefly use my charm
On creatures that do people harm
On mole and toad and newt and viper
And they call me the Pied Piper.

Instrumental break in which the Piper does a dance holding out the pipe as if it
were an imaginary partner

I come from a land that is far away
Full of mystic tales of joy and dread
We wear long coats, half yellow half red
And my pipe—strange music it can play.

And I chiefly use my charm
On creatures that do people harm
On mole and toad and newt and viper
And they call me the Pied Piper.

Dance

Last year in Tartary I freed
The land from flying, swarming gnats
And I rid from Asia vampire bats
And for you—I'll do whate'er you need.

And I chiefly use my charm
On creatures that do people harm
On mole and toad and newt and viper
And they call me the Pied Piper.

Dance

Give me a task that bewitches or bewilders
That no other man has been able to do
I'll raise my pipe and I'll do it for you
And my charge—is but a thousand guilders.

And I chiefly use my charm
On creatures that do people harm
On mole and toad and newt and viper
And they call me the Pied Piper.

Dance that ends with a bow

Mayor	A thousand guilders is the price?
Piper	Your rats will vanish in a trice.
Mayor	We'll pay you more if you succeed.
Piper	A thousand sir, is all I need.

The Townsfolk cheer

Drumroll/electronic sounds

The Piper prepares. He clears a circle—the Townsfolk watch from the sides, intrigued to see what the Piper will do. He holds his pipe like a dagger up to the north, south, east and west, then spins round. But the Priest does not move

Priest   (*over drumroll*) Wait! Be careful! I sense danger
God tells me not to trust this stranger
If you meddle with his magic
The consequences will be tragic.

The Townsfolk react nervously. Thunder clap

The Piper slowly brings the pipe to his lips ... He pipes three long mysterious notes. Gradually the Children "become" Rats again and one by one are drawn towards the Piper, unable to resist the charm of the music. This is choreographed to the song below

Music 12: Listen to the Music

1st Rat   Listen to the music from this fellow
(*singing*)   In his strange coat of red and yellow
Follow
Come follow
Let's follow him

1st Rat and 2nd Rat sing together

1st rat	**2nd Rat**
Follow	Listen to the music
Come follow	From this fellow
Let's follow him.	In his strange coat
	Of red and yellow
Follow	Follow
Come follow	Come follow
Let's follow him.	Let's follow him.

2nd and 3rd Rats sing together as above

Rats sing in canon ...

Rats   Listen to the music from this fellow
                  In his strange coat of red and yellow
                  Follow
                  Come follow
                  Let's follow him.

All Rats   Brothers and sisters, husbands and wives
                  Let's run with the Piper for our lives
                  Follow
                  Come follow
                  Let's follow him.

                  Forget your sorrows, forget your grumbling
                  Come out of the houses jumping and tumbling
                  Come along now and take your chance
                  Let the Piper lead a merry dance.

                  Listen to the music from this fellow
                  In his strange coat of red and yellow
                  Follow
                  Come follow
                  Let's follow him.

*The last three lines are repeated as the Rats follow the Piper round the stage
and perhaps round the auditorium. Eventually they arrive lined up across the
front of the stage, walking on the spot*

*The Townsfolk gingerly move to a vantage point behind the Rats. The Piper
stands to the side*

The Policeman unobtrusively exits to prepare for his "Old Rat" entrance

*Rats keep repeating the last three lines of the song, in a whispered fashion until
directed to stop. Over the top of this ... the Townsfolk narrate in unison*

Townsfolk   On and on, they could not stop
                  'Til in the river all did drop.

*Dramatic lighting change and sinister electronic sound effects to accompany
... The Rats mime in slow motion drowning in the river. The Townsfolk watch
in amazement. The Piper smiles. The Rats finish up dead in the "river". The
Townsfolk are elated*

                  The rats are drowned, hip, hip hooray!
                  Let's make today a holiday.

Music 13: One Foot Up and One Foot Down (Reprise)

(*Singing*)   There's a law in Hamelin Town
                  That none of us should wear a frown
                  We laugh all day and sing and play
                  And down by the river we stroll and say

Chorus
One foot up and one foot down
That's the way in Hamelin Town
Now the rats have gone away
All we'll do is sing and play
So join our dance in Hamelin Town
One foot up and one foot down.

Silence

Music 13a

After a pause an "Old Rat" enters exhausted; He breathlessly chants the "Follow, come follow" song. He wears an "old rat" half mask

The Piper watches

Old Rat surveys the scene, sees the dead rats, reacts appalled, then escapes, running off as the music swells

Music 14 (Reprise of Music 11)

(In the original production the reprise of Music 11 was recorded, all but the "and rats" line, which was spoken live; this heightened the atmosphere)

The Lights fade. The voice of the Piper echoes eerily through the darkness

Piper   And I chiefly use my charm
  (singing)   On creatures that do people harm
                       On mole and toad and newt and viper
  (speaking)   And rats
  (singing)   And they call me the Pied Piper.

The Piper laughs—a sinister chuckle—and vanishes into the shadows

Black-out

ACT II

A quiet opening

The Old Rat enters

Old Rat   I s'pose I'm lucky, I have my life
But I lost my children, I lost my wife
Of all the rats I was the last
Because I couldn't run as fast.

We heard a sound so strange and distant
Calling each and everyone
Magic music so insistent
Willing us to run and run.

To a kind of rat Utopia
Where we'd live a life of ease,
Promise of a cornucopia
Of butter, biscuits, cake and cheese,

Caviare and pâtéd liver
Apple pies and candied grapes
Then we reach the raging river—
Except for me no rat escapes.

I s'pose I'm lucky, I have my life
But I lost my children, I lost my wife
Of all the rats I am the last
Because I couldn't run so fast.

A drum beat starts

The Old Rat reacts and runs off. (NB: He should return almost immediately as the Constable)

Music 15: We Can Whistle, We Can Play

The Townsfolk enter happily singing a celebration song. It is as if they are outside a pub and have been celebrating in drink for some time. The song develops into a clap/slap dance

Townsfolk   We can whistle, we can play
(singing)   We can dance all through the day
The birds they sing, the bells they chime
Every day's a happy time.

We can whistle. We can play
We can dance all through the day
The birds they sing, the bells they chime
Every day's a happy time.

Constable   Now's the time to celebrate
Mother   The rats are gone we used to hate
Mayor   We feel happy, we feel free
So come now bring some food to me

All react with laughter to this line

Townsfolk   We can whistle we can play
We can dance all through the day
The birds they sing, the bells they chime
Every day's a happy time

Dance. The Constable leads the dancing by starting off with a variation of the "Fool's Jig", using his truncheon as a stick. The dance is then joined by the Townsfolk

We can whistle, we can play
We can dance all through the day
The birds they sing, the bells they chime
Every day's a happy time.
The birds they sing, the bells they chime
Every day's a happy time.

The Piper enters

The Townsfolk all gather round the Piper to cheer him and thank him

Mayor   Welcome, sir, congratulations.
Come and join our celebrations!
Piper (*quietly*) Celebrating's not for me
I would simply claim my fee.
Mayor (*as if*   A fee? A fee?
surprised)   You claim a fee?
Piper   A thousand guilders . . .
Mayor   That can't be!
You must think me some buffoon
To pay so much for just one tune!
Piper   No trifling, I must be gone by noon.
Mayor   Besides, our business was done at the river's brink,
We saw with our eyes the vermin sink
And what's dead can't come to life, I think.
But, friend, we're not the folk to shrink
From the duty of giving you something to drink
But our losses have made us rather thrifty
A thousand guilders? Come, take fifty!
Piper   I only want my just desserts
1st Voice   Yeah! Give the lad his just desserts

The Priest pushes through the Townsfolk

Priest	And what pray are the just desserts
	For one who does the *Devil's* works?

The Priest points an accusing finger at the Piper. The crowd gasp

1st Voice	The Devil's works!
2nd Voice	The Devil's works?
	Good Priest why say you so?
	He's kept his word and saved the town!
Piper	My fee—then I will go.
(to the Mayor)	
Priest	Do you think payment should be made
(to the crowd)	To one who's used High Magic's aid?
	Who puts God's creatures in a trance,
	Beguiled by magic pipe and dance?
	Pay gold for sorcery and charm?
2nd Voice	But, sir, he did nobody harm.
Piper	Call it magic if you will
	But I prefer to call it skill,
	A secret skill from dawn of time
	Which you would now declare a crime
	(Pointing to the Priest)
	Yet when *your* prayers your God had spurned
	To *my* ancient skills *they*
	(Pointing to Townsfolk)
	gladly turned,
	So

The crowd watch the argument like a tennis match

(To the Mayor)	I warn you once, I want my fee.
Mayor	Get out! How dare you threaten me!
Piper	I warn you twice to keep your word.
Mayor	Away! This whole thing's just absurd.
Piper	I warn you thrice—the rats have gone.
Mayor	Oh yes, but magic's surely wrong.
	(He turns to the crowd)
	If we let witchcraft rule this place
	Who knows what danger we could face?
	If we pay this man, be sure
	We could be damned for ever more!

The crowd pauses to think. Muttered discussion. Then ...

1st Voice	Beat him!
2nd Voice	Duck him!
3rd Voice	Let him drown!
Constable	Wizard! Out! Get out of town!
Townsfolk	Out! Out!
(chanting in	Turn him about,
unison)	Catch the wizard
	And chase him out.

                              Out! Out!
                              Turn him about,
                              Catch the wizard
                              And chase him out.

Piper
(*with a*   Sto . . . . p!
menacing
echoing cry)

The Townsfolk recoil

(*In sinister,*   Folk who put me in a passion
controlled   Will hear me pipe in different fashion.
tones)
Mayor   You threaten us? Then do your worst
                    Blow your pipe until you burst.

Music 15a

Electronic music (or drum roll)

Piper   By all the power of land and sea
(*declaiming*)   By oak, by ash and bitter thorn,
                     For breaking of your pledge to me
                     You'll rue the day that you were born.

Pause

1st Voice   Out, out, and don't come back!
2nd Voice   Catch the wizard and break his back!
3rd Voice   Out! Out! Out!

The following section is a psychic battle, a ritual challenge between the Townsfolk and the Piper

Townsfolk (*in*   Out!
unison, advanc-
ing towards
the Piper)

The Piper spins once, anti-clockwise, on the spot, and at the end of the spin, extends his arms out towards the Townsfolk as if to return their curse. The Townsfolk step back and recoil

(*Advancing*   Out!
again)

The Piper reacts as before. The Townsfolk recoil

(*Advancing*   Out!
again)

The Piper reacts as before. The Townsfolk recoil

The Constable briskly advances, takes the Piper by the arm and escorts him off

Narrator   Now the Piper and the rats had gone
Normal life could carry on.
Joyfully the church bells rang
As the townsfolk danced and sang.

Church bells peal and continue throughout the following song

Music 16: One Foot Up and One Foot Down (Reprise)

Townsfolk   Ev'ry day's a holiday
Now the rats have gone away
We stroll along the riverside
And no-one else can match our pride.

One foot up and one foot down
That's the way in Hamelin Town
Life's too short to work all day
All we do is sing and play
Join our dance in Hamelin Town
One foot up and one foot down.

Music continues under the narration

Narrator   The days went by, the weeks went by,
The months became one year—
One year exactly since the day
The rats did disappear.

Townsfolk   There's a law in Hamelin Town
(*singing*)   That no-one ever wears a frown
We laugh all day and sing and play
And down by the river we stroll and say

Chorus:
One foot up and one foot down
That's the way in Hamelin Town
Life's too short to work all day
All we do is sing and play
Join our dance in Hamelin Town
One foot up and one foot down.

Bells ring out joining the last few lines of the song. As before in Act I they change at the end to a death knell toll, which continues during the following narration. Lighting slowly fades to Black-out on the final words of the song

  The Townsfolk exit

Death knell bell continues

Narrator   The townsfolk had forgotten how
(*through*   Their saviour they did spurn
darkness)   But late that night, by blue moonlight
The Piper did return ...

The bell stops. Lighting comes up as at the beginning of Act I

The Piper is discovered, in silhouette, centre stage with his back to the audience

Music 17: Boys and Girls Come Out to Play (Minor version)

The Piper starts to play the slow and eerie version of "Boys and Girls Come Out to Play"

As the Piper plays, the Lame Child enters dressed in a long white night-gown. She listens to the music for a while, then sings the minor version of the song

Lame Child   Boys and girls come out to play
The moon is shining as bright as day
Come with a whistle and come with a call
And come with a good will or not at all.

The Lame Child then turns and beckons on the other Children and sings:

We've all been called to come and play
The moon is shining as bright as day
He's come with a whistle, he's come with a call
He wants us to follow so come along all.

The Children enter, one by one, wearing white night-shirts or night-gowns and all walking sleepily, as if entranced by the music

The Children sing a round of the minor version of the tune, so therefore are in two groups. The round is structured so that Group Two start to sing as Group One sing the word "out", in the first line

Children   Boys and girls come out to play
The moon is shining as bright as day
Come with a whistle and come with a call
And come with a good will or not at all.

The Children join hands and walk slowly, in time to the song

Children
(in unison)   Boys and girls come out to play
The moon is shining as bright as day
Come with a whistle and come with a call
And come with a good will or not at all.

During this last verse the Townsfolk enter (without Priest) and mime trying to take their Children away from the Piper

There is a mimed struggle. The Children keep singing and circling around regardless

Townsfolk
(random cries) Children, what are you doing out here?
Come home!
You should be in bed.
What are you doing? Come away!
Wake up! Listen to me! ... *etc.*

The Piper stops playing and points the pipe at the Townsfolk, waving it like a magic wand, rooting the Townsfolk to the spot. Now they cannot move, only watch. The Children laugh manically at their parents' predicament

The Piper starts to play again. He leads the Children in and out of the Townsfolk. The Children sing in unison the major version of the song. As they do so the Children point and gesture tauntingly at the Townsfolk. The Children appear very happy

Music 18: Boys and Girls Come Out to Play (Major version)

Children   Boys and girls come out to play
The moon is shining as bright as day
Come with a whistle and come with a call
And come with a good will or not at all.

The chorus is repeated as necessary. Perhaps the Piper leads the Children to the "river". A dramatic pause as it appears he may force them all to drown. But then the music starts again and the Children resume their singing, following the Piper

The Piper continues to play the tune, as he leads the Children off-stage, possibly through the auditorium. The Children are still singing or humming

The Lame Child noticeably lags behind the others and when only she is left on the stage, or in the middle of the auditorium . . . She sings happily, the tune still in major mode

Lame Child   The moon was shining bright as day
He called us all to come and play . . .

The Lame Child exits excitedly after the others

The Townsfolk, still unable to move, remain. Lighting gradually fades up as dawn rises. The Townsfolk are still transfixed

The Priest enters and walks in and out of the Townsfolk looking closely into each face

Priest   Dark forces walk throughout the land
This has the mark of the Devil's hand.

He stands in front of the Townsfolk and raises his hands to heaven and intones

    Matthew, Mark, Luke and John,
Bless the ground that they stand on.
By candle, Holy book and bell
Wake them from this magic spell!

The Townsfolk slowly start to move, shaking and scratching their heads in a dazed manner, as if waking from a deep sleep

1st Voice   First I heard a gentle sound
Like waves that lap upon the shore,
2nd Voice   Then I heard a frightening sound
A mighty, rushing roar,

3rd Voice	Strange music chilled me to the bone
	And turned my limbs to stone.
Priest	By God's good grace you are now free
	But tell me how this came to be.
1st Voice	Last night when the moon shone brightly down
	The magic Piper returned to town
2nd Voice	And as we, at home, lay fast asleep
	Our children from their beds did creep,
3rd Voice	He played his pipe and they danced away
	It's the curse he made that fateful day
	We drove him out without his fee
1st Voice	It's a punishment for all to see.
2nd Voice	
(*pointing to*	It was you that told us what to do
the Priest)	
3rd Voice	So our children are gone because of you!
Priest	Oh! No!
	Your children aren't lost because of me
	Nor lost because of a Piper's fee!
	I warned you of your dangerous game
	You've no-one but yourselves to blame-
	"If you with the Devil play
	Then you must the Devil pay."

The Priest turns on his heel and exits

The Townsfolk group round to console each other. The Mother steps away from the rest and looks distraught

Music 19: Mother's Lament

Mother	Oh! where is my child
(*singing very*	My pride and my joy
slowly)	Oh! where is he now my own darling boy?
	He was so fond of dancing
	And he loved a fine tune
	He followed the Piper
	By the light of the moon.
Townsfolk	They followed the Piper
	By the light of the moon.
Mother	Oh! where is he now
	My joy and my dove
	Oh! where is he now my own precious love?
	Will he ever return
	Safe home to my arms?
	Will he stay with the Piper
	Beguiled by his charms?
Townsfolk	Will they stay with the Piper
	Beguiled by his charms?
Mother	Oh! where is my child

My pride and my joy
Oh! where is he now my own darling boy?
He was so fond of dancing
And he loved a fine tune
He followed the Piper
By the light of the moon.

Townsfolk   They followed the Piper
By the light of the moon.

The Townsfolk move to the Mother and comfort her

The Lame Child enters opposite the group

A single spot finds the Lame Child. The main Lighting dims

Lame Child   No, mothers, your children did not die
It's true you'll never see them more
But they're not dead you can be sure
Listen and I'll tell you why.

We followed the Piper through the town
Under his spell, unable to fight
And as the river came in sight
Like the rats, we thought we'd drown.

We felt no fear, just joy and hope
The Piper gave us his protection
Then suddenly he changed direction
And led us up the mountain slope.

And as we reached the mountain's side
A wondrous portal opened wide
As if a cavern was suddenly hollowed
And the Piper advanced, we children followed,
The door in the mountainside shut fast
When all were in to the very last . . .

Except for me, for I am lame
I couldn't keep up with the dance
And so I lost my only chance
And life will never be the same.

The Townsfolk exit

It's dull in our town since my playmates left
I can't forget that I'm bereft
Of all the pleasant sights they see
Which the Piper also promised me.

Music 20

The Children enter, still in nightshirts and nightgowns. They stand behind the Lame Child who cannot see them. The Children form an angelic chorus.

Back lighting to suggest that they are in some form of paradise. They speak in unison

Children   He led us to a joyous land
                    Joining the town and just at hand
                    Here waters gush and fruit trees grow
                    Here sunshine streams and sweet winds blow
                    Here flowers put forth a fairer hue
                    And everything is strange and new
                    The sparrows are brighter than peacocks here
                    And the hounds run swift as fallow deer
                    The honey bees have lost their stings
                    And horses are born with eagle's wings
                    A place of magical atmosphere
                    And we are always happy here.

The Lights fade from the Children who exit

The spot stays on the Lame Child

Lame Child   But just as I became assured
                    My lame foot there would soon be cured
                    The music stopped and I stood still
                    And found myself outside the hill
                    Left alone against my will
                    To go limping as before
                    And never hear of that country more.

Music 21: Mother's Lament (Reprise)

(Singing   Oh! where are they now
unaccompanied) Oh! where do they play
                    Oh! where are they now
                    Can they hear what I say?
                    They so loved the music
                    They so loved the dance
                    They followed the Piper
                    They joined in the dance.

She goes on humming the tune as she slowly exits

The Mayor enters and during the following final section of story-telling narration, the Townsfolk and Children, back in modern costumes, enter and take up their positions in the tableau last seen in Act I when the play within a play started

The Lighting remains dim

Mayor   The Mayor sent East, West, North and South
                    To offer the Piper, by word of mouth,
                    Silver and gold to his hearts content
                    If he'd only return the way he went
                    Bringing the children behind him
Narrator   But no-one could ever find him.

Church bell begins a death knell

> And when they finally understood
> Their children all had gone for good
> The scene of the children's last retreat
> They called it, The Pied Piper's Street—
> Where no-one was allowed to play
> A note of music, night or day
> Except the church bells' solemn chime
> Reminder of that tragic time.

The Mayor removes his "chain", becoming the Business Man again. The Lighting returns to daylight. All are now reassembled. The Townsfolk address the Small Child, still sitting watching

Vicar And this, my child, is the very street.
Lollipop Lady Pied Piper street.
Mother (*to small child*) So, now you understand, don't you, why you can't sing or dance here.
Business Man Because of what happened to those other children long ago.

The Small Child nods and joins the others

Policeman (*to the Piper*) And that's why, I'm afraid, I have to ask you to move along, sir, and play somewhere else.
Tradesman Stands to reason.
Piper (*standing*) A fascinating story. When did it happen? On what day of the year?
Vicar The Feast of St John.
Piper And what day is it today?
Business Man June the twenty-fourth.
Vicar (*realizing*) The Feast of St John!
Piper Exactly, sir, the Feast of St John.

Music 22

Electronic sound for tension. The Piper smiles enigmatically. The Lighting begins to change to the mysterious light in which we first saw him

Lollipop Lady (*nervously*) What's going on?
Vicar It can't be. It's impossible.

Music 23

The Piper starts to play—the eerie minor version of "Boys and Girls Come Out to Play." After a pause ...

Tradesman (*in amazement*) He's come back.
Business Man Come back? Nonsense. It's some kind of joke. Things like that don't happen in this day and age!
Policeman (*firmly*) Come on, that's enough!

The Townsfolk watch powerlessly, as the Children slowly stand and, mesmerized, approach the Piper

Vicar No! Children! Stop! Stop!

The Children begin to dance, the same slow-motion dance they danced at the beginning

Mother Come back! Come back!

The music speeds up and the Children dance more energetically, forcing the Townsfolk to back away

Lollipop Lady Stop him!

The Policeman tries to reach the Piper

Policeman (*shouting*) Stop playing! Stop that music! STOP!

But he cannot get through the frenetic mass of Children. The Business Man grabs the Policeman and whispers urgently to him

   The Policeman hurriedly exits

Business Man (*shouting*) Listen please, listen! Please stop! Stop! (*Desperate*) STOP!

The Piper stops

The Children freeze in ecstatic dance positions

Piper (*calmly*) Well?
Business Man Please. Leave the children alone.
Piper I offer them Mirth. Merriment. Life!
Business Man Yes, but listen. You haven't heard the end of the story yet.
Piper This, sir, *is* the end of the story. This *is* the end. (*He goes to play again*)

The Townsfolk gasp

Business Man No, listen, please. You see, all those years ago, after the Pied Piper . . . after *you* had gone, the townsfolk felt guilty. Oh yes, they were angry too, and overcome with grief at the loss of their children. But they felt guilty.
Vicar Ashamed at how unfairly they had treated you. You had cleared the rats. You should have been paid.
Piper True.
Business Man So a collection was made. A thousand guilders, the full fee. All these years it's been kept at the Town Hall, by generation after generation, just in case the Pied Piper . . . *you*, should ever return.

The Policeman enters, carrying an old-fashioned bag, full of money

Policeman (*formally*) Here it is. Please accept this and the formal, sincere apologies of the townsfolk of Hamelin. (*He gives the money to the Piper*)

All wait on tenterhooks. After a pause, the Piper smiles. He should now be standing centre stage

Piper   Now at last you've paid my fee
                   And Hamelin from my curse is free.
                   You've learned your lesson,
                   You've paid the score,
                   And you will never see me more.

With a click of his fingers, he magically releases the Children from his spell

The Children unfreeze and nervously back away from the Piper, to the arms of the waiting Townsfolk, who shoo the Children off-stage, then quietly exit themselves

The Lighting narrows to just the Piper

Music 24

The major version "Boys and Girls come Out to Play" is heard played on the Piper's pipe (perhaps recorded)

Music 25

Reprise of Music 11 chorus

(*Singing*)   And I chiefly use my charm
                On creatures that do people harm
                On mole and toad and newt and viper
                And people call me . . .

The Piper turns, facing upstage. He freezes in the position seen at the beginning of ACT I

The recorded echoes of children's laughter fade up and up and up . . . Suddenly both light and sound snap out

Black-out

Music 26: We Can Whistle, We Can Play (Reprise)

After the cast return to take their curtain calls, the music strikes up for a final reprise of "We Can Whistle, We Can Play", or, if more is required, a medley of reprises, consisting of "We Can Whistle" (Music 15), "One Foot Up and One Foot Down" (Music 5), "Boys and Girls Come Out to Play" (Music 18) and finishing with "The Pied Piper's Song" (Music 11)

FURNITURE AND PROPERTY LIST

ACT I

On stage: Nil

Off stage: Pogo stick **(Child)**
Doll's pram with doll **(Child)**
Bicycle, chain, padlock **(Business Man)**
Lollipop stick **(Lollipop Lady)**
Toolbox **(Tradesman)**
Stuffed cat on invisible thread **(Townsperson)**
Pot and brush **(Ratcatcher)**

Personal: **Piper:** pipe (required throughout)
Policeman: truncheon, whistle
Old Rat: half rat mask

ACT II

Off stage: Bag of money **(Policeman)**

Personal: **Old Rat:** rat half mask
Lame Child: crutch
Policeman: truncheon, whistle

LIGHTING PLOT

Property fittings required: nil

An open stage

ACT I

To open: Very subdued blue lighting

Cue 1	As electronic sound gets louder *Fade to black-out*	(Page 2)
Cue 2	When ready *Bring up lighting—bright daylight*	(Page 2)
Cue 3	At end of **Music 5:** death knell tolls *Dim lighting*	(Page 5)
Cue 4	**Both Groups** (*rising to a climax*): "... Rats, rats, rats!" *Black-out*	(Page 7)
Cue 5	**Rats** exit *Bring up lighting*	(Page 7)
Cue 6	**Townsfolk:** "... all did drop" *Dramatic lighting change*	(Page 17)
Cue 7	**Music 14** *Fade lights*	(Page 18)
Cue 8	**Piper** vanishes into shadows *Black-out*	(Page 18)

ACT II

To open: General lighting

Cue 9	During last few lines of **Music 16** *Slowly fade to black-out*	(Page 23)
Cue 10	Bell stops tolling *Bring up subdued blue lighting*	(Page 23)
Cue 11	**Lame Child** exits excitedly after the others *Gradually increase lighting as dawn rises*	(Page 25)
Cue 12	**Lame Child** enters *Spot on Lame Child; dim general lighting*	(Page 27)
Cue 13	**Children** enter and form angelic chorus *Back lighting to suggest paradise*	(Page 28)

Cue 14	**Children:** "And we are always happy here"	(Page 28)
	Fade back lighting on **Children**; *hold spot on* **Lame Child**	
Cue 15	**Lame Child** exits	(Page 28)
	Fade spot on her; keep lighting dim	
Cue 16	**Mayor** removes "chain", becoming **Business Man** again	(Page 29)
	Increase lighting to daylight	
Cue 17	**Piper** smiles enigmatically	(Page 29)
	Change to mysterious lighting	
Cue 18	**Townsfolk** shoo **Children** off, then exit	(Page 31)
	Narrow lighting to just the **Piper**	
Cue 19	Recorded echoes of children's laughter fades up and up	(Page 31)
	Black-out	

EFFECTS PLOT

ACT I

Cue 1   **Children** fall down, all expelling a great sigh   (Page 2)
         Strange electronic sound, increasing in volume

Cue 2   Black-out   (Page 2)
         Cut sound

Cue 3   **Townsfolk** hold end-of-song/dance pose   (Page 5)
         Death knell toll—fade as narration starts again

Cue 4   **Townsperson** runs off to the wings   (Page 12)
         Mewing, off

Cue 5   The **Townsfolk** cheer   (Page 16)
         Electronic sounds

Cue 6   The **Townsfolk** react nervously   (Page 16)
         Thunder clap

Cue 7   **Townsfolk:** "... all did drop"   (Page 17)
         Sinister electronic sound effects as **Rats** *drown*

ACT II

Cue 8   During last few lines of **Music 16**   (Page 23)
         Death knell toll

Cue 9   **Narrator:** "The Piper did return"   (Page 23)
         Stop bell

Cue 10   **Narrator:** "But no-one could ever find him"   (Page 29)
         Death knell from church bells

Cue 11   **Mayor** removes "chain", becoming **Business Man** again   (Page 29)
         Fade bells

Cue 12   **Piper** turns, faces upstage, freezes in position   (Page 31)
         Fade up recorded echoes of children's laughter—increase, then
            suddenly cut as Lights snap out

MADE AND PRINTED IN GREAT BRITAIN BY
LATIMER TREND & COMPANY LTD, PLYMOUTH
MADE IN ENGLAND